Wind Age, Wolf Age

Hugh Crago

Wind Age, Wolf Age

Wind Age, Wolf Age
ISBN 978 1 76041 461 0
Copyright © text Hugh Crago 2017
Cover photo: Trish Davies

First published 2017 by
GINNINDERRA PRESS
PO Box 3461 Port Adelaide 5015 Australia
www.ginninderrapress.com.au

Contents

Preface	9
Academies	**11**
The Timeless Land	13
Saint Cecilia's Musical Academy	15
Mentor	19
Sixty-something	23
Wood Between the Worlds	25
Be Ashamed to Die	28
Gustav Mahler: Symphonic Lessons in Death	32
The Presenting Past	**35**
'Ready about!'	37
Envoi (*Sir Gawain and the Green Knight*)	40
Dark Watchers: Velasquez's *Las Meniñas*	43
Rejoice Greatly: Handel's *Messiah*	47
'Who Will Tell The Emperor?'	48
Lenin in the Toyroom	52
Somewhere in America	56
Aspirational Lifestyles	**61**
Seven Out of Ten Are Affected	63
'Take Me Away!'	65
Calling Cards	68
Bliss Was it in That Time	70
If (academic style)	75
'An Inspired Statement in Contemporary Living'	77
Ghost Whisperer	79
Dream Country	**81**
The Climb	83
You're Always Alone in Your Dreams	84

Inside Out	86
Snow at Sea c. 1790	88
The Lavatories of Night	89
Ride the Orange Bike into the Room of Surprises	91
How Dreams Grow Old	92
Nacht und Nebel	95
Traffic Lights in Fog	97
Nacht und Nebel (Night and Mist)	99
Snowfall	101
Wind Age, Wolf Age	102
First Meeting with the Button-moulder	104
Towards Winter	107
Windy Night on the Lower North Shore	109
Sweet Lassitude	111
So Comes That Time	113
De Senectute (After Cicero)	114
I Sit In a High Place	116
Walking Into Rain	117

Vindøld, vargøld, aðr verøld steypisk
'A wind age, a wolf age, before the earth expires'
Icelandic *Poetic Edda*, c. AD 900

Preface

In 2009, at the age of sixty-three, I suddenly began writing poems. I'd previously published other writing, but had never thought of myself as a poet, or aspired to be one. I'm still not sure why this happened, but I think it had more than a bit to do with my stage of life – a key theme in the poems collected here. As we age, the right hemisphere of the cerebral cortex – which perceives the world in vivid, here-and-now images and startling connections, and which *sings* rather than speaks, may return to its early childhood dominance over the left hemisphere's rather one-dimensional rationality. For me, at least, poetry has become a natural mode of expression once again.

The earliest poems I produced were fierce jabs at the many things that irritated me about the world in which I now lived. Some of them have survived in the section of this volume that I've called Aspirational Lifestyles. Others (*Nacht und Nebel*) were responses to the harsh beauty of the upper Blue Mountains, where my wife and I have lived for the past seventeen years. An increasing number (Dream Country) took their inspiration from the cinema of the unconscious (I sometimes wake from dreams with intriguing images, and a line or two that later turns into a poem). But most of all, I found myself writing about old age (Towards Winter). It's not a popular subject for writers generally, nor is it likely to find a wide audience among younger readers, who are understandably reluctant to look too closely at what is to come.

Of course it's hard not to feel gloomy when your body (and sometimes your mind too) won't do any longer what it used to do. But growing old is not all gloom. Part of it is vividly remembering key experiences in your childhood and youth, and that's the subject of the poems in the sections called Academies and The Presenting Past – and, indeed, all the way through this volume.

I would like to thank my wife Maureen. That some of these poems have pleased her has meant more to me than I could say.

Hugh Crago

Blackheath, 2017

Academies

The Timeless Land

Artarmon, 1956; Canberra, 2014

Beyond the faded Persian rug
On which he has disposed
Old, felted playing cards
In line abreast and line ahead
Like ships or soldiers –
Beyond that miniature classroom
In which, just ten years old,
He schools himself in history,
Its fateful decisions and
Inevitable catastrophes –
Lies something else,
Ungraspable, hovering on
The horizon of consciousness,
A lost city at the close
Of every quest, a blue bird
Beyond the rainbow's end.

Perhaps it is a neon-lit, metallic
Future, whose moving walkways
Elevate him smoothly
Into the steely realm of adulthood,
Where spaceships dart
Like hummingbirds
Between tall buildings?

Perhaps it is a past, sealed tight
In boxes redolent of camphor
Which, when opened,
Unleash the storm of time
Where random objects –
Discarded epaulettes, envelopes
Whose stamps bear wartime overprints –
Stir in a cold and dusty wind
Of hurtful things once voiced
And painful thoughts unsaid?

Yes, somewhere over the rainbow,
As yellow brick gives way to glowing green,
Before Atlantis sank beneath the sea,
There is a corridor of entrances,
Each clearly signposted,
Yet every one, he'll learn,
Leads only to that timeless land
Where a child, just ten months old,
Longs urgently to pass
Into a wondrous garden
In which the cats walk free
But he can only gaze at them
Through glass.

Saint Cecilia's Musical Academy

Grafton, 1959–63

My father's non-conformist church
Had long abjured the hierarchy
Of heaven, but then I met
A saint – Cecilia – face to face,
In Burne-Jones colour, hanging
Over the piano. It wasn't long
Before I'd drop the 'Roman' too.

My father's father had (I later found)
Detested and distrusted Catholics,
Impressed on Dad abhorrence
Of *statues and holy pictures –*
That sort of thing, which proved
(To Grandfather, at least)
That 'RCs' (as he called them)
Worshipped idols. Dad
Was broader-minded, and besides,
He cared for music, and wanted us
Well taught – and so we rode
Our bikes to Saint Cecilia's,
Free-wheeling and back-pedalling
Through Grafton's broad and silent streets
Where jacarandas perfumed the humid air
To the house outside the convent gates
Where the sisters plied their trade.

Augustine taught my brother – generally kind,
She had her moments, though.
Cecilia, the youngest and the sweetest
Taught my sister and, some said, had
The best piano; but I, as eldest, got
The senior teacher, Raymond, and
Consequently got converted –
Not to the One True Church,
Holy, Catholic and Apostolic,
But to those other persons
Of the Trinity: self-discipline and shame.

Raymond's name didn't sound much
Like a Saint's, and she was
Older than the other two (at twelve
You aren't that good at picking adults' ages).
She was no sadist, like nuns I'd known
Before – ruler poised to crack
The knuckles of a boy who didn't elevate
His wrists, with fingers drooped correctly
Above the keys –

No, Raymond wielded subtler instruments,
The lure of honours in exams,
The fear of stern rebuke when pupils
Failed to measure up:
I *should be ashamed*, she said,
And I'd *disgraced my father* too.

Five years of forcing fingers
To alternate correctly,
Five years of hands apart and
Hands together, till at last
Quotidian components
Became perfected whole,
A transubstantiation I
Could comprehend.

The satisfying final chords,
The brilliant shimmer of a trill,
The melodies that rose like streaming rocks
Above the waves of their accompaniments,
The dying falls, the sudden peals of triumph –
I loved it then, felt lifted up, a part
Of something larger than myself.

But like Sebastian, pierced by arrows,
Or Catherine, torn upon her wheel,
I learned that pain must come before
Ascent to everlasting life, dark suffering
Precede the burnished disk of sanctity.

I learned from Sister Raymond to expect
Much of myself, and when I taught in turn,
I would expect the same of those I taught:
Precision, care, respect for words,
Deference to dogma, persistence,
And a fierce dedication to the task
Of making flesh conform to duty.

I learned these things from her
And yet, of course, I knew them all before.
Discipline was there, and shame, waiting
Since infancy to take their place
On either side of God the Father Almighty,
Judging the quick and the dead.

I knew that 'quick' (in King James' prose)
Meant 'living', but made my own translation:
My practised fingers *could* move fast, earn praise:
Slow hands meant shame – a little death
Reminding me that *diminuendo ad finem*
Applied to other things than music.

Mentor

The University of New England, Armidale, 1964–69

For Professor John Ryan, 1929–

White, he wore white (or cream, perhaps?) –
That's what I noticed first:
Tropical jackets, matching pants,
And highly polished shoes in brown.
The others called him Jungle Jim
Or Jungle but I chose to call him
J.S.R. That's how they spoke
At Oxford – where he'd been,
And where he'd met the man
Who dreamed of Hobbits
In a garage lined with books –
A man who was, it seemed, a dandy,
Wore cream suits – I got the point.
(Tolkien mumbled, too, and rambled,
People found him hard to understand,
But J.S. didn't mention things like that.)

Behind the lectern, J.S.R. held forth:
Words flowed like the Anduin
That separates Rohan from Gondor,
Ideas were *adumbrated* (it meant
Foreshadowed) and images
Were *numinous* – charged with
Spiritual significance. His lectures
Were a *palimpsest* of Alexandrian
Allusions new and old, and the commentary
Often swamped the text.

His college rooms, a book-lined cave,
Became an island where a former duke,
Wielding wisdom, justice too,
Offered stern rebuke to airy spirits
Like myself, in love with academe,
But ignorant as Caliban of what
An academic's calling really meant.

The man himself was sometimes miserable,
Longed for love, a wife and kids,
A home outside of college.
Betrayed by the academy he served,
And wary of his colleagues,
He walled his cave more stoutly,
Bought more books, and wrote them,
Acquired two doctorates to other scholars' one –

Yet Sycorax refused to be confined.
He saw in me – I know it now – a younger
Self, yet not himself: that difference
Was an irritant. He was the scholar
I was not, but aimed to be; I was
The writer he was not, but craved to be.
I too was passionate and yet
Restrained by codes I only half
Believed. I too spoke out
In outrage, willing to upset
The kings and princes of our world,
And so we exiled ourselves
To similar islands.

He was the father I would not
Let my own dad be,
The sharp-tongued, disillusioned
Mum I knew too well –
The old king underneath the golden bough,
Awaiting his successor's axe.
I raised that axe, not knowing what I did.

Years after,
I would wear
The same cream clothes,
Type stories in a garage full of books,
Parade my arcane learning
With defiant confidence,
And mentor students in my turn.

Like J.S.R. I'd come to realise
That honours, recognition
And promotion counted less than faith –
The faith we had in those we noticed,
Nourished, then sent out,
In envy and in love
To better us,
Become us.

Sixty-something

In 1960-something
I began to wake
From cosy childhood
Into hope and hate.

Lead singers screamed
Into their bulky mikes,
Speakers ranked behind,
Black mountains like
The guardians of Mordor.
Guitarists keened and wailed
At one one zero decibels.

Below the stage,
The crowds of gentle freaks
Turned violent, a placid inland sea
Transformed into tsunami.
A distant war in black and white
Was *just a shot away*, in colour now.

As 0069s, we started to awake
Into a childish kind of adulthood,
Independent but irresponsible,
Licensed to mock (but not to kill)
The law-men who committed
Us to murder in humid
Jungles far away, haunted
By the rotor blades of
Slowly turning ceiling fans.

F-111s, shitting napalm,
Painted evergreens with rosy orange
Bringing fall in old Vermont
To steamy Vietnam.

In 1960-something we were not
The first to think we'd change
The world, but like Sam Coleridge
In 1790-something, we had
Vision without persistence,
Moral righteousness –
But not the necessary realism.

The Cone of Silence would descend
Upon us, KAOS would survive
To die another day, the Wall
Would fall, but hate would last,
The death of Robespierre
Was only the beginning
Of terror's war on us.

In comfortable middle-age
We settle for a maintenance dose:
Beguiling daydreams
Of sunny pleasure domes
That never were
And never will be.

Wood Between the Worlds

Neate Park, Blackheath, New Year's Morning, 2010; Oxford, 1969

Here, in the long-tamed east
Of the northern world's deep south,
A hesitant old continent has briefly shrugged
Its shoulders – apologetically introducing
Plateau land as mountains which nonetheless,
On sunny days, shine Lost Horizon blue,
Their sandstone ramparts glowing gold.

Physicians, lawyers, publishers,
Who fled to this hill station to escape
Relentless summer on the coastal plain,
Embellished their Black Heath
With rhododendrons, planted avenues
Of northern trees so they could wade
Through crackling heaps of leaves,
Just as their parents had, when autumn
In another country turned their breath to smoke.

As pines they'd planted
Soared emerald against a sky
Intensely blue, they must have felt
They had the best of both –
The present's heat on eucalyptus leaves,
The misty past where snow
Lay deep and crisp, if only
In the Neverland of memory.

Today, the newest year in my own sixty-odd,
A sudden stillness holds its peace.
The roaring highway's bare of trucks,
No wind disturbs the trees that dot the park.
The grass, close-shaven, sweeps
Toward the empty rails. Beneath
A sky pregnant with impending rain,
The foliage distils its green as if
Imprisoned sunlight yearns
From every glossy leaf.

This waiting parkland spells
My mind back forty years,
Compelling me like green or yellow
Rings forged by a magician
Who thinks he's using them, when all along
They're using him, for purposes his art
Is powerless to help him see.

A bright young man walks thoughtfully
Across another close-mown park, but this one's in
A northern land's long-settled south.
He notices wet foliage against the low
Grey sky, the golden sandstone walls
That loom out of the lawn, blackened
Not by Cromwell's cannon, but, ignobly,
By industrial smog. The ancient city
Disappoints, the wisdom
Of the well here at the World's End
Confers no everlasting life, and
Charles' Royal city cannot stand.

In 1969, this young
Man's pact with Mephistopheles
Will buy him forty years of wasted life.
Snow leopards will not show because
A writer needs them for his book,
Shangri-La recedes behind its peaks,
The blue bird flutters out of reach.

But now, in twenty-nine, at least he knows
Enough to see the point of all those tales:
It's glancing light that makes a blue bird's
Plumage blue (its feathers, separately,
Are yellow-brown). The green appears so green
Because the sky is grey. Their meaning's
Where they are, not somewhere else:
Here, in this reverential now.

This is the power, the pact, the spell:
Live by it while you can endure.
The blue bird's *here* in summer, pecking seeds
From dried-out backyard lawns, *there*
Beneath the oaks in autumn's chill,
When leaves lie heaped
And mist obscures the marshy ground
And all around is still.

Be Ashamed to Die

Keene, New Hampshire, 1979, Blackheath, New South Wales, 2010

'Be ashamed to die until you have won some victory for humanity' was the motto of Horace Mann, founder of Antioch College (now Antioch University), which began teaching in Yellow Springs, Ohio, in 1852. Our campus in 1979 was Antioch/New England Graduate School, and has since become Antioch University, New England.

Viewed from the air, the hills
Of south New Hampshire
Are furred with forests, farmland
Limned with winding walls,
Streams spanned by bridges
Roofed against the winter snows:
Frost's country; more recently
Jed Bartlet's too (idealism isn't dead
As long as it's still credible on TV shows).

Ninety miles south of Keene
Is Boston, whence a man called Mann,
One-hundred-fifty years ago,
Rode out west to found a college.
He called it after Antioch – the place
Where Paul preached Christ
To sceptical, sophisticated Greeks –
But Mann, a latter-day evangelist,
Had secular conversion on his mind,
Bade future graduates be *shamed*
To die until they'd won
Some victory for human kind.

When the 1960s briefly flared
And revolution seemed to gather pace,
Mann's Antioch caught fire,
Inspired new radicals,
Consumed the continent –
Reached Australia, far enough
To gather us to its embrace.

We came here, thirty years ago –
Ten years since Altamont had ended
The Woodstock dream, two hundred
Ten since Paris burst the gates
Of the Bastille.

Antioch sat quite uneasily
In tidy Keene, New Hampshire, then.
With their own college, Keene's folk snubbed
This questionable import from Vermont.
Even faculty good-humouredly agreed:
*Antioch in Putney, man—it was
Flake City!* What more damaging
Admission could the locals want?

Our school was crammed into
A small square building, painted blue,
Behind the Square, spilled over
Into North Street, and if
The ground-floor loos
Spilled over too (*Bad news! Don't use!*)
We suffered in absolute equality
And fraternity.

You see, the spirit counted, not the letter,
The inspiration, not the accommodation,
And when New Hampshire license plates
Proclaimed *Live Free or Die*, we knew
They weren't invoking just
Defiance trumpeted to tyrants
Like King George. The words
Beckoned us to change through *love
Not war*, a *velvet revolution*.

To Antioch came rebels, every kind –
We had idealists to burn
(Not literally of course), and hot debates:
Could the Feminists
Admit a token man? And if
If you came too late for Group,
Did fellow Groupers have
The right to shut you out?

Political correctness, in its time,
Had been responsible for Salem and
McCarthy (*I saw Arthur Miller
With the Devil!*). But at A/NE, the ideology
Was more benign. Wars were waged
With words, not weapons, the scale
Was individual, and mass destruction,
Even to safeguard public safety,
Was way outside the line.

We came, we were accepted, fitted in.
We fell in love, and fell apart,
We lived and breathed the heady
Air of interpersonal intensity
For two brief years, until
For us, came time to start
Again, back home.

*

Now, half a world away, the bulletins
From Antioch still come – in colour too.
They bring, as through a telescope,
Tiny, distant scenes of what we knew:
New bridges built, old walls dismantled,
Change, like melting snow, seeping
Into winter fields, and in them all
Unchanged compassion,
An undefeated hope.

Gustav Mahler: Symphonic Lessons in Death

1965–2010

When I was twenty, the Second commanded me
As crudely as those SS men, arms outstretched
Towards their leader – a black parade of death
That somehow ended in a blaze of primal light,
In which the voice of God boomed
From the organ's metallic throat:
Whoever falls
Will rise again
You have not lived in vain!

It was, perhaps, a little overstated:
This short, ambitious convert
Gestured too grandiloquently. But I
Was young, and just like Mahler, craved
The large and obvious (eight braying horns,
Eight snarling trombones). I heard
The Ninth too but it seemed
An endless wandering
In boggy wilderness,
Petering out in marshlight.

Twenty years went by, and then
It was the Sixth that sang into my mind:
Mahler's knight rides forth, no callow youth,
A veteran of life's wars, knowing what he knows.
He turns his steed onto the mountain paths:
Tinkling bells, the plaintive call
Of flute and oboe, remind him what
He's left behind: the fertile plain,
The many-lighted city.

Then,
Inexorable,
The blows of fate:
Great
Hollow
Thumps.

The last one
Strikes him down.
The symphony
Expires.

No Christos Pantocrator,
No Valkyrie to lift him
To Valhalla.
A hero's death
Is just a death
Like any other.

Now I'm sixty, it's the Ninth
I need to hear. I see
My father's uncle, struggling
To shave himself, just days after
The stroke that laid him low,
Compelled to look his part until the end.
Mahler, too, is struggling – his heart
Demands death duties in advance.
Into his mind seep feelings from his youth:
A woman's musky scent, the nostril-flare of fame.
But life is leaching from him, day by day.

Two middle movements dance frantically
Against inevitable entropy,
Then Gustav Mahler ceases to deny.

Death seeps around the edges
Of the fourth and final act,
Woodwinds twitter in the growing dusk,
And strings breathe in and out
Without a pause, slowly
Loosening their grip
On life until, at last, one faint
Continuing note is all that's left –
Or is it there at all? –
A space once occupied by sound.

The Presenting Past

'Ready about!'

Arthur Ransome's *Swallows and Amazons*

For Dave Straton and Peter Hunt

In that safe time before
Sex substitutes its servitude
For more innocent devotions,
I drew endless pictures
Of clippers running
Their easting down,
Or homeward bound
From China, sometimes
Clocking up to twenty knots
When winds called trades
Blew steadily for days and weeks.

Somehow I knew I too
Was built of fragile wood
Not solid steel, dependent on
The winds to fill my sails,
Built for speed, and scornful of
The need to stuff my holds with
Dirty, necessary coal.

I tried to build those vessels too –
From balsa wood and dowel rods,
Their towering masts decked out
With neatly ordered sails.
Alas, my ships capsized –
They lacked the keels
That should have reached
Beneath the water to offset
Those heavy masts above.

In adolescence, I avoided
Arthur Ransome's world, where
Kids my own age, equally immune
To sex and death,
Guided their 'Swallow' and 'Amazon'
Expertly round English lakes –
They didn't mean to go to sea;
It made them adults, suddenly.

Years later, forty-odd, I found
A friend who'd grown up in that world,
He took me with him on his boat
And taught me patiently to watch
The sail's edge, put the tiller over
(Ready about!) when the canvas
Flapped, taught me how to steer,
And how to shift my weight to
Balance the wind's insistent pull.

I think he hoped to offer me a metaphor:
To take my cue from wind and wave
Instead of my anxieties.
I didn't get the point back then,
While he was bored with little boats
And wanted something bigger:
'Swallow' drifted far from 'Amazon'.

Years later still, poems
Began to come, welling up
Like water from an uncaulked seam,
Bearing me on their surge like great
Swells towering behind my stern:
I had to trust my boat to them,
Avoid a panic turn, beam-on,
Which would have left me swamped
And sinking.

Now, on this whale-road of words
That carried Beowulf to Heorot,
This wine-dark sea that took the
Greeks' black ships to Troy,
My little boat bobs about –
And every now and then
Comes up into the wind
So sweetly I could sing.

Envoi (*Sir Gawain and the Green Knight*)

Sometime late in the fourteenth century, the anonymous poet who
composed *Sir Gawain and the Green Knight* addresses readers of the future*

Something about this story sticks in the mind.
It puzzles and teases, perturbs while it tantalises –
Steel plate gleaming through shot silk.
It won't let go of me, however long I try
To turn my thoughts to patience, purity, and proper
Christian concerns: despite prayers it persists,
Pagan, yet promising a partial resurrection.

No saints this time, no pious pearls we'll thread
But war and woe and wonder,
Monsters and marvels, the green axe
That shocks us into dread.

Pagan, yes, product of those who peopled the land
In times long past, the ones we pushed
Over the seas, beyond the Romans' wall,
To live in their accustomed ways, unknown to us,
Singing their sagas of Cuchulain and cauldrons
That oddly echo our own, we must admit,
Though ours come straight from God and theirs (we're told)
Direct from hell. But who's to say which of the two
Will live the longer, light the land six hundred years from now?

When Richard's reign is past
And broom no longer flowers
When Bastard's blood runs thin
This story's bloom will last.

A comedy you'd call it, not one to make men laugh,
But rather to delight the wits of those with wit to bring,
Pitting courage against terror, courtesy against temptation,
Christian piety against uncanny powers,
Virtue riding against the boar of lust, hunting down
The fox of fear. A tale to divert those who go to mass
With wandering minds, who kneel to take the Host,
Their thoughts on worldly passion, not on Christ's.

If Gawain's tale can lure
Their souls to honour's rod
Then goodness may absolve them
Although they flee from God.

And you, beyond time's blue, foreshadowed hills –
How will you see good Gawain's chronicle? A fairy tale, fit
Just for children? Castles cut from cardboard,
Paper knights and green-faced ogres?
Or a challenge for your clerks, perhaps – close scholars,
Poring over each part, questing for the key,
Threading the maze to the *real* Green Chapel?

My story's both, and neither.
Make of it what you will,
But hearken while it speaks its truth
So it bring you good, not ill.

Take it with you, looped securely round your loins,
Into whatever fearful future you may face.
Who knows? It may remind you of your sins,
Sins I cannot name or know, and bring you safe
And almost sound, to your own Green Chapel.
It comes to all of us, that bleak midwinter day –
Do you not hear the whirring from above?

When Camelot is but a dream
And I a man long dead
Still ringing sharp within the hall
You'll hear the Green Knight tread.

---

*Sir Gawain and the Green Knight was written in lines 'with coupled consonants constructed', that is, where at least one word in the first half of each line alliterated with at least one word in the second half. The unrhymed stanzas ended with a four line 'tail', written in short lines that rhymed. 'Envoi' roughly approximates this metre, which looked both backwards to Old English alliterative poetry and forwards to French-influenced rhymed verse as preferred by Chaucer.

Dark Watchers

Velasquez's *Las Meniñas*

The crowded chamber soars into the dark –
The shadowy paintings on its walls,
Like *tercios* close-ranked behind their pikes,
Refuse to yield to our inspection.
An unseen window to the right permits
Pale sunlight to illuminate some people
Grouped for us to watch.

The girl-child's little face pouts slightly,
Jaw thrust forward as a Hapsburg's should,
Her head, atop the armoured bodice
That confines her slender chest, held high
With unselfconscious pride. In womanhood
Such bodices will keep her bosom flat,
Her wired and stiffened hair will stretch
Beyond her shoulders, as the hooped
And stiffened skirt conceals her hips:
No sinful lift of firm young flesh
Will be allowed to sway her senses
Or tempt improper thoughts from those
Below her elevated station.

On either side of their Infanta,
Meniñas, maids-in-waiting,
Young women chosen for their birth,
Ensure their Princess' golden hair
Is orderly, positioned so it traps the sun,
Instruct her not to smile or speak
Without command. Thus is the dignity
Of kings maintained, Spain's glory
Burnished bright, a golden gleam
Across the water from the Old World
To the New.

No matter that the Treasure Fleet
Is mortgaged to the last *escudo*
Before it ever leaves the port
That bears God's Holy Name,
No matter that the *tercios* retreat
Across the Low Countries,
That upstart heretics and Huguenots
Disturb the certainty of Catholic kings:
Still customs must be followed,
Due processes observed, for these
Keep fear in check. The end
Of Spain, the end of kings may loom,
But such a thought's unthinkable.
Pray, act fittingly, God will provide.

Another woman, face aged early
By the accident of birth, stares, stoic.
A king's dwarf knows her station –
No courtier, but of the court, a place
Beyond the reach of any common dwarf.
Likewise the boy in crimson at her side,
The hound at ease upon the floor,
The couple standing in the shadows
Beyond the window's pool of light.

Furthest away, a modest figure
Dressed in sombre black leans
In a lighted doorway, draws
Aside the arras, gazes at their backs.
All know their proper places,
Know whereabouts to look, and
What they can and cannot do and say –
But where are we within this room?

We are mere ghosts. We have no rank,
No place, no lineage. We are as insubstantial
As the masses said for Felipe Segundo, wiping out
The sins that he committed in his life,
Ensuring kingly credit after death
On purgatory's soul-ledger.

I, Don Diego de Silva y Velazquez,
Extend this privilege to you, dark watchers
From beyond the Ocean Sea of time:
I give you this one moment in the life
Of princesses and dwarfs, of kings and hounds,
Caught in the sunlight, as spring
Begins to melt the snows of old Castile.

Rejoice Greatly

Handel's *Messiah*

Is it possible that time
Within this sound-Versailles –
Its ordered gardens, gilded halls,
Elaborate cornices – folds cunningly
Upon itself, like carved acanthus leaves?

Might these our faces, in the steady light
Of electricity, merge with others,
Flickering in candlelight?
Our deodorised, clean bodies
Smell like theirs, of musk and sweat?
Amidst the rustling of wigs and ruffled sleeves,
Are we too leaping to our feet,
Our 'Bravos!' rivalling
The trumpet's soaring notes?

My father would have said
He knew that his redeemer lived,
But would his faith have died
Without this music, comforting
His people, then and now?

Behold a mystery:
For these two hours
Is every valley raised,
Each rough place made plain,
The raging of the nations halted.
And when our bodies sink to dust,
These notes remain,
Exalted, incorruptible.

'Who Will Tell The Emperor?'

Artarmon Railway Station, June, 2009

In June 1942, the Imperial Japanese Navy launched an ambitious attack on Midway Island in the Pacific, CIC Yamamoto's real aim being to destroy America's three operational aircraft carriers, which had escaped Pearl Harbour six months earlier. Two thirds of Japan's carrier strike force, commanded by Admiral Nagumo, were committed to the battle, but the Americans had broken the Japanese code, enabling them to anticipate Yamamoto's plans, and to inflict a disastrous defeat.

If you think about it
(Which you probably don't)
This small suburban station
On the North Shore Line
Looks a little like
A carrier.

Seen from above, steel lines swirl
Along *Artarmon*'s flanks, as if
Carved through waves at thirty knots.
Its flight deck tapers at the bow,
Swells amidships to accommodate
Its 'island' – the stationmaster's office.

Trains slow as they approach the platform,
Like planes coming in to land, but
We don't turn this carrier into the wind
To launch our trains, nor, when they gain speed
Do they ever ditch into the sea –
Only a passenger's occasional
Kamikaze dive, I guess.

At peak hour, there's people running,
Leaping aboard as doors slide shut.
New trains pull in just minutes after
Their predecessors launch.

Human bodies everywhere,
Orderly when things go to plan,
Hopelessly exposed if anything
Were to happen. But nothing,
Surely, will ever happen here?

*

Nagumo's four carriers
To the US's three,
Veteran pilots, Zero fighters
That could outfly
Any aircraft in the world:
Midway should have been
Another triumph for
The Empire of the Sun.

But Nagumo's canniness
Deserts him – crowded by choices,
Deprived of data, his platforms littered
With torpedoes, fuel lines, and planes,
He changes his decision yet again.
At 7.45 a.m., US bombers swoop
And tear apart his decks
As easily as origami.
Akagi, Kaga, Soryu, great floating fortresses,
Death Stars of a time before Luke walked the skies,
Are burning, listing, gone.

Hiryu scrambles from the smoke,
Launches a forlorn last strike. Her planes
Wound *Yorktown*, but returning, find
Their home ablaze. Yamaguchi
Composes appropriate verses
As he strides his bridge, waiting for *Hiryu*
To take him down.

Oh say, can you see
By the dawn's early light,
How hundreds flail helpless
As the burning oil licks them?
The thousands trapped hopeless
At the twilight's last screaming?

Far off, Yamamoto,
The one who'd fiercely
Opposed this war, now knows
His own Pearl Harbour:
Kito Butai: destroyed.
Midway invasion: aborted.
The mad dream ended
As he always thought it would.
His mind turns homewards:
Who will tell the Emperor?
He, Yamamoto Isoroku, knows
His duty as a samurai.

*

Here, in June sunlight, after sixty years,
No metal sharks menace our hull,
No fighters strafe our waiting crowds,
Instead of bombs, pamphlets
Advising us of global warming
Blow uselessly around the platform.

Eight thousand people daily crew *Artarmon*,
A flightdeck full of vulnerability.
High above, in cloudless air,
There looms the far-off threat
Of an uneasy future
And the Emperor's not answering
His emails.

Lenin in the Toyroom

'Leuralla', the Blue Mountains retreat of the Evatt Family, now houses a toy and railway museum

Under stately trees, raised high
Above the close-mown grass,
Vladimir Ilyich fixes Capital
With a fierce gaze, as if
His train had just rolled in
To Petrograd (listen and you'll hear
The distant sound of clanking shafts,
Imprisoned steam released).

The Doc was twenty-three the year
That forty-something Lenin
Made his fateful journey home – a
A young man on the move, stoking
His firebox with ambitions and ideals.
By '45 the way ahead seemed plain:
The Fascists gone, a clear-eyed future
Would replace a dark and bloody past.

Now Lenin and the Doc,
Once-great and would-be great,
Together haunt this park
Of past preoccupations,
Their ideologies unreal to us
As ancient theological disputes
That people killed each other for.
In 1453, a Christian Emperor's city fell
And changed its name to Istanbul.
Now Lenin's city, which survived in '41,
Is once again Saint Peter's.

The Evatts' house is solid, white,
Two-storied, home to people
Born to privilege, but animated
By the wish to carve a better life
For those who weren't. They
Came here yearly to escape
The weight of office, the clamour
Of the House, the Court – the speeches made,
The judgements handed down.

The bedrooms where their children slept,
The sitting rooms in which they talked till late,
The halls and stairwells once alive
With hope and laughter, now are crammed
With dolls and tiny trains, a century
Of toys.

Here Barbies stand
In serried ranks like Cybermen,
Sporty dolls clutch tennis racquets,
Princess Elizabeth holds the hand
Of younger Margaret, Biggles
Flies the skies in uniform green cloth,
Dan Dare cleans up the universe
In gaudy rocket ships, along with
Tintin, Snowy and James Bond,
While Honor Blackman's naked form
Lies gilded on a plastic couch.

But look again: this cabinet of curiosities
Contains deep contradictions –
More indeed than Meet the Eye.
In Toyland Munich,
Model S.A. men march past
A celluloid *Braun Haus*.
Their Führer stands erect,
His plastic arm outstretched,
As if he'd never put that heavy
Pistol to his head. Whose children
Played with this? And how has it
Survived his *Götterdämmerung*?

What other children, in some bungalow
Within the Civil Lines, took out
From this capacious box such perfect
Replicas of elephants and envoys,
Maharajas and mahouts, colonels and
Commissioners, hundreds waiting
To be assigned allotted places
As the King-Emperor, robed and magisterial,
Takes the salute under the canopy
That shields him from a sun
They never thought would set?

No tiny, skulking figure yells defiantly
Quit India! Yet the world of that Durbar
Has gone, annihilated as effectively
As Hitler's thousand years of Aryan glory.

What happened to the boys who made
These mighty structures of Meccano?
Did they build bridges, scrape the skies
Above New York? Did youngsters
Of the Komsomol unpack heroic
Labourers and red-starred riflemen?
Or was the need for tanks
Too great for metal to be spared?

Toys, so scholars tell us, whisper to our children
Who we hope they'll be: Barbie and Ken
The Perfect Couple, James Bond – the spy
Who loves you for one night;
Rupert, the polite boy-bear who cracks
Enigmas for his village; Biggles,
Battling von Stahlheim forever.
Jumbled together in this place of puzzles,
They confront us – as we age without
Them – with the shrinking of ambition,
The rusting of ideals, the relativity
Of faith.

Somewhere in America

Ray Bradbury's *Something Wicked This Way Comes*; HBO's *Carnivale*

For Fred Goldsworthy

Somewhere in America
A white frame house,
An upper storey window.

Edward Hopper painted it,
Standing open in the early light,
One morning in Maine.
Raymond Chandler, in
An L.A. Summer, saw a stiff
Lying on the bed that Hopper's dame
Had just vacated.

In Mississippi, Caddy Compson
Climbed back through this window
After tangling with a boy.
Billie Faulkner, the would-be
Boy she tangled with,
Stared through it at his grandmother,
As she lay dying.

Somewhere in America,
A white frame house,
An upper-storey window
Open to a summer night,
A coming storm.

The boy who sits in it is
Wide awake. A sudden breeze
Rattles the panes, mixes prairie dust
With the fierce, sharp smell of rain.

Out there, somewhere in America,
The fair is coming, coming –
Menacing, magical,
A match's rasp in the dark,
The cool thrill of her hand on
Your face, speaking of desire
You don't yet recognise
(Too young for her, they told him).

Maybe it's the *Carnivale*,
Run by a good-natured dwarf
Under orders from management
(A soft-voiced demon
Behind a curtained alcove
In that caravan you dare not go
Unless you're asked).

Oh, it's *The Greatest Show on Earth*
With all the sights you didn't really
Want to see, but had to know about:
The Bearded Lady, delectable
And smooth below her hairy chin,
The Illustrated Man, his body
Tattooed within an inch of his –
Never let me hear that word again!
The naked girls, defiantly displaying
Their teenage breasts (as if they
Didn't do it every night
In this hot tent, while
Gawking youths grin knowingly,
Hearts racing, wet with sweat).

Somewhere in America –
This gentle, brutal country
Sitting huge amidst its contradictions
Like Lincoln throned upon the Capitol –
A boy like you sees lynchings,
Murdered whores and guns discarded,
Jungles flowering with liquid fire
(*Too young for him, they told her*),
Arthur sleeping with Morgana,
Guinevere betraying him
With Lancelot, Uncivil War
And Grand Theft Auto everywhere
From sea to shining sea.

Yeah, somewhere in America
A window's open to the night,
And though it's high above the ground,
Something wicked has parted
The drapes your mother made
When you were little, and
Slipped silently inside.

Aspirational Lifestyles

Seven Out of Ten Are Affected

Sydney Town Hall Station, May 2010

Enthroned at Sydney's heart, Victoria –
Queen, Empress, grieving widow –
Stares blankly at the winter rain,
Stolidly prepared to do her duty,
Though dead a hundred years.

Deep underground, on platform five,
Two schoolgirls meet, crafting
An embrace as stiffly separate
As if *Heil Hitler*ing. Their frozen
Smiles across each other's
Shoulders stare at other kids
They're sure are judging
Their performance.

From billboards opposite,
A model, twice life-size, stares blankly
At our smaller bodies staring.
She's advertising *Wish*
(The line is sold by David Jones)
And so we know what we should wish for:
A face like hers – devoid of joy
And pain, blank eyes animated
Only by the camera's flash.

Another billboard (black and white
To indicate it's *information*)
Tells its readers seven out of every ten
Of us are touched by mental illness,
Which, we learn, embraces grief
As well as schizophrenia,
Mortgage stress as well as mania.

'*Be prepared,*' said Baden-Powell,
Founding the Boy Scouts
Before we'd heard of paedophiles
Or patriarchy. Well, we're prepared:
We check the train times on our phones
Instead of glancing at the board above,
The online weather's more reliable
Than looking at the sky. We text
Our friends, make sure they're
Watching on the Book of Faces.

Frail beings, self-created by
Our butterflying minds,
We're on our way from somewhere
We've forgotten to somewhere
We don't want to know.
Meantime, though:
Big to-do list?
Stay pumped!

'Take Me Away!'

Hugeness, the Ancients knew, lifts us
Above ourselves, inspires thoughts
Of power, quest, transcendence.

Assyrians built avenues
Of monstrous bulls with
Curled and tinted beards
Like the Great King's in Nineveh.

In Egypt, Pharaoh's statues
Dwarfed tiny Asiatic enemies;
A giant lion-bodied man kept guard
Before his everlasting tomb.

Maya sovereigns like Eighteen Rabbit
(Perhaps the Sun King of his time)
Required the climbing of stairways
To heaven, tier on steep-raked tier,
Until, with each breath rasping,
Chosen ones attained the summit where
The priests stood waiting, knives
Obsidian-edged, bearing
Bowls to catch their blood.

The high-rise buildings in our CBDs
Still touch the floor of heaven, they
Compete for light like giant redwoods
In a concrete glade –
But nothing's at the top. No kings
Hold sway in their penthouses,
No sacrifice is needed, only payment for
The ritual feast at the revolving restaurant,
The ritual contemplation
Of the city view. Prawns,
Not gods, get torn apart.

Yet as the white cruise ships glide in and out,
Some trace of awe and glamour hangs
About them. Giant bulwarks curve
Above our heads, ranked portholes
Stud the snowy sides, the decks stretch on
Towards the edges of the globe,
Promising other worlds beyond
The brick veneer and Colourbond
That define our daily tedium.

Only the elect, of course, perceive
The bargain: absolution bought
With blood. Most think only of
The endless ecstasy, of sex
With temple prostitutes
Who slide into your cabin and
Expertly embrace you – and your mates –
In sacred copulation that might
Quicken corn, if this steel and plastic
Boat of Ra had any corn to grow.

But in their darkened cells
Beneath the towering, white
Ziggurat, the priests remain:
Old Gods demand
Their sacrifices still.

Calling Cards

Dogs lift their legs and urinate –
Leave calling cards, acknowledge
Those of other dogs:

Mrs Robert Kirkham.
At Home.
Third Thursday.

The mingled smells – some cooling,
Some on heat – perhaps convey
Sophisticated narratives
Of love and loss:

Prince Andre was here.
Killed in action.
Pierre 4 Natasha.

Likewise our species' young
Tag every wall with signatures
Conveying to the literate in cuneiform
A formal grandiosity:

Great King,
King of Kings,
King of the Four Quarters
Of the ~~World~~ Western Suburbs.

We toss away the evidence
Of hamburgers consumed,
Drop neatly-packaged baby poos
Along the gutters as
Our latest-model cars fart past.

We strew the Internet
With Hansel's crumbs, telling
Predatory wolves and paranoid Dads
What we've done, and
Who we did it with.

We need to tell each other
Who we are, and who we've eaten,
How wiped out we were,
And how much fun that was,
Affirming that we're just as individual
As every other person in the crowd –
A Mission Statement dogs
Would surely understand.

Bliss Was it in That Time

Bliss was it in that time to be alive,
But to be young was very heaven
See William Wordsworth's *The Prelude*, 1805

On giant plasma screens
Above, try-hard chicks
Shrill lyrics in voices
As tight as their tummies,
As tiny as their shorts.
Digitally enhanced, they
Hide their spotty doubts
Under pancake positive thinking:
They're *in the zone*.

For us, hair was Nature,
Sexy too (*unreal!*)
A gentle challenge to
Short back and sides for him,
A lacquered perm for her.

We grew our hair, Rapunzel-like,
In unisex profusion.
Greying harpies hissed
You can't tell which one is the girl!
Loud enough for both of you to hear.

Now hair's become a turn-off
In every sense, it seems:
Kill, kill, exter-min-ate.
Actually, the fashion Daleks let it live,
But only under strict controls.

Men shave it down to stubble
(That pink, bumpy
Skull gives a whole new meaning
To 'dickhead', doesn't it!)
Women chop it cruelly short,
Dye it lurid orange, purple
Or make damn sure they wax
It off entirely in Brazilian areas.
Sex with no hair is sexier, it seems.

We wore untidy beads,
Medallions, ankhs, adopted
Gender-neutral greetings (*Peace, man!*).
Now, it's 'dude' and 'bro'.
And pink bits, apparently,
Are 'hotter' if pierced with studs
And rings (for us, rings led
Their bearers to Mount Doom.)

We wore purple, scarlet,
Lace and leather fringes. Our
Old Ladies abandoned underwear.
Freed by the Pill, exploding in fountains
Of foamy joy (*Blow my mind!*),
We were manic – these days they suffer
Agitated depression.

Fashion Roundheads,
They've reverted to tight black,
High heels, that mincing walk
Originally produced
By the corsets we despised:
Well, they say, you gotta
Walk the walk
If you wanna
Talk the talk.

Sixties music wrecked
Our tender ears, but it had
Rhythm as well as blues,
Melody as well as metal.
Theirs is only loud. You
Caint get no satisfaction
When the rhythm never varies,
When the lyrics just go round and round
In electronic loops, and even drums
Are made by a machine.

Get in the Tardis,
For God's sake, and travel
Somewhere else!

Easy riders, born to be wild,
We knew our brave new world
Would somehow reconcile
Clean surf and the T-Bird's
Roaring exhaust, walls of giant
Amps and butterflies
Above our nation, Shelley's 'Adonais'
And the storm-cloud chords
Of *Gimme Shelter*.

But free love left us sadly
Unfulfilled, you can't
Run comfortably without a bra,
The music didn't bring a paisley-patterned
Revolution. The Eighties were
No place for a street-fightin' man:
Before we knew it, we'd become
Ageing hippies, risible actors in
That Sixties Show.

Now there's plenty still to fight,
And plenty to fight for,
But it's *funner* to
Film yourself playing
Air guitar on You tube,
Make a virtual fortune
In *Second Life*, kill virtual enemies
In *World of Warcraft*
And live in other people's dreams
To avoid the nightmares of
The warming world you live in.

But, when they in turn grow old,
They'll inhale nostalgia
Like the day's first cigarette,
Convince themselves *they* lived through
Revolution, pin the ribbon
Of respectability on their coats,
Compose a techno 'song':

'Bliss was it in that time
Bliss was it in that time
Bliss was it in that time
That time to be alive,
That time to be alive
That time to be alive…'

If (academic style)

University of Western Sydney, 2009
After Rudyard Kipling's 'If'

Wise people speak slowly – or used to –
But now how smart you are is measured by
How quickly you can talk, how many
Clauses (*And, there's more!*)
You can subordinate, until your listeners
Are panting with the effort to keep up.

Today's dons spit it out so fast
You'd swear they're selling alloy wheels
And air bags, not Foucault and Derrida.
At conferences they gabble through
An hour's worth in twenty minutes,
Relieved when no one challenges, although
It's disappointment they pretend to show.
They've sworn the oath of cleverness:
Always speak in complex words
If simple ones would do.

Ah yes, they've let themselves be herded here
Dismissed their own forebodings.
Here, within the neat brick walls,
In the wooden huts behind the wire,
It's *Publication Makes You Free*
(well, free to publish even more).
Forget weekends, forget the kids – you're here
To work or die. Keep your head down
So the guards don't see you,
Or act as *Kapo* to your fellow *Untermensch*.

Podcast your lectures—little chunks
As full of juicy meat as if they're made by Pal –
Get that website up, let students
Rate your teaching every year, rush
That application in, ditch your unspent dollars
Before the grant runs out. Maybe Kipling,
Self-righteous, racist bastard though he was,
Did get one thing right:

If you can fill the unforgiving minute
With 90 seconds worth of Po-Mo porn,
If you can twist wisdom into cleverness
Turn wonder into scorn,
You'll be the very model of a modern academic
And what is more –
You'll be a Prof, my son.

'An Inspired Statement in Contemporary Living'*

The soft-skinned, white-haired folk
Don't greet you when you pass,
Just glance, then go on weeding.
Their garden beds have concrete rims,
The soil is bare and free of anything
But neat petunias, little clumps of box
All ready for their monthly perm.

Young mothers push their prams
Along a leafless pavement,
Edged with fresh-mown turf.
Nice girls avoid your smile, assume
Blank faces, stride ahead with confidence
Towards the pool, the gym, the coffee shop.

Their bungalows are cool and dark –
Two stout brick walls, a cavity between.
Beethoven can sing of Joy in triple f
Inside, but outside not a sound.
There's no disorder here, it seems,
No random shouts or shots,
No smashing glass, no personal effects
Tossed on the manicured front lawn
To mark the end of trust.

Surrounded by *the ambience of yesteryear*,
On *spacious, level blocks*, the denizens
Of Sydney's North Side live
Their *inspirational lifestyle*, waiting for
Supremely comfortable deaths.

* Real estate agent's billboard outside a property in Burra Road, Artarmon, March 2011

Ghost Whisperer

Wallowing in sleep-surf, dragged
Under by the rip of dreams,
I surface in the hour when even trains
No longer run. Unaccustomed silence
Enhances every sound, and yet
Unmoors its meaning.

From somewhere – a
High window in Marlowe's
Los Angeles? A street outside
A Crows Nest bar? –
The voices start.

I can't distinguish words although
Their shape suggests FUCK YOU!
And yet the screams are loud
Enough to seem close by. It's no
'Domestic' though –
The cast is clearly large.

I wonder if it's just TV
Turned up too loud –
Some desperate housewives
Confronting husbands' infidelities,
Crime scenes investigated
To reveal a grisly burial
Beneath the kitchen floor?

Or is it real? (Whatever 'real' is,
When we learn to chuck
A *hissie fit* from scripted
Confrontations? When reality
TV sounds *unrealistic*
Because its lines are
Unrehearsed?)

Can any profiler be smart enough
To work this M.O. out? Can Dr Paul
Or Dr Phil resolve this codependent
Triangle in treatment?
Who ya gonna call?
These ghosts may shout at us
But we have lost our voice:
We merely whisper in return.

Dream Country

The Climb

The narrow stairs rise steeply,
Curve to left and right:
You climb them just
Because they're there,
Because you must:
The end is out of sight.

Taut with excitement,
Breathing hard, you reach
Another landing, stare
Above you at the final flight,
The glow you're sure is there.

Years later comes the fear,
The doubt: someone below you,
Creaking; someone above you,
Waiting: but the slope is sheer,
There's no way out.

Your climb is laboured now
And slow. Still you must reach
The top. There may be nothing –
Only endless stairs – or worse:
A blackness and a drop.

No matter what you still may
Have to learn, to see or hear,
It's all you know
And you can't stop.

You're Always Alone in Your Dreams

The studio of waking life is crowded
With obligations and anxieties,
Conversations that rattle
Round my head, but my dreams
Are filmed on location
In a land that only old
Surrealists recall:
Departure lounges lined
With empty plastic seats, grey
Escalators rising endlessly
To shuttered shopfronts
In monochrome malls.

I share a house with a wife
And two dogs but dreams
Accommodate me on
A silent corridor –
Single rooms
Inhabited by single men,
All out in search of sleaze.

I type away in cafés
Wallpapered with songs
From thirty years ago, while
Plates rattle, and steam hisses
From the espresso machine.
I'm inches from the
Table next to me but I'm alone.

Yes, there is another world
But uninhabited:
When your shuttle touches down
In its grey dust, the only alien
Is yourself.

Inside Out

Lost highways at night –
The muffled roar of trucks
Approaches and recedes –
A passing light
Flickers round the park,
Invites me out into
The urgent dark.

A sudden squall
Lashes the glass,
Shakes insubstantial walls:
Rain dissolves to mist.
A shiver down my spine:
The outside's yours
But the inside's mine.

Warm weight against me,
I touch your thigh
I'm hard and eager –
You're inert.
The bed still reeks
Of the scent of whores:
The outside's mine
But the inside's yours.

The darkness sleeps,
The lights go by,
The rain drips sullenly,
The traffic roars,
Our bodies lie,
Breathe in time:
The outside's yours
But the inside's mine.

This poem grew out of a phrase that was the sole survivor of a now-lost dream: 'The outside's yours/But the inside's mine'. The rest of the poem was built around images from David Lynch's movie *Lost Highway*.

Snow at Sea c. 1790

Inspired by images from a dream in 2016

And then, towards midnight,
Snow began to fall upon
The black and heaving sea.
Swirling frenziedly at first,
But as the wind left our sails,
Fat flakes sank slowly down
To coat the shrouds and
Crust the wooden walls
That cradled us.

We did not know, then,
What it meant, and yet
We sensed a peace
Beyond our comprehension,
A temporary truce,
A momentary light –
The flicker of a lantern
Reflected in the heaving
Water far below.

The Lavatories of Night

Public toilets have a certain lack of charm:
Rows of silent cubicles, ill-fitting doors,
Harsh disinfectant struggling
With the stink of piss;
Imagine, though, ablution blocks
In high-rise form, at night.

Successive floors, each one
Equipped with basins, toilets,
Shower stalls – deserted
Under unforgiving lights.
This is what my dreams
Insist upon, despite the fact
I've never seen such things:

Empty stairwells where
My footsteps echo loudly.
When I pause, I hear
The sound of running water:
Ever-flushing urinals,
And cisterns voiding
Even as they fill.

I leave the stairs and walk
Uncertainly into the open space:
No neat rows here, but cubicles
That open into others, tiles
Slippery with the flow
From brimming toilet bowls.
In vain, I walk from stall to stall.
Find nothing uncontaminated.

More stairs lead down
To yet another floor equipped
For multiple ablutions but
Deserted now. This time, though,
The toilet bowls are dry, bone-dry.
Their cisterns hang with long-gone
Spiders' webs. The shower heads
Are rusted up, with only brownish
Stains to show where final drops
Once dribbled to the dusty tiles.

Well, nothing here. Dispirited,
I step back, and the stairs
Once more lead steeply down…

We all know dreams make movies
From our bodies' aches
And urgencies – but dreams don't
Just direct to someone else's script.
They're *auteurs*, with pretensions –
Declare their independence
Of the feelings and memories
They're quarried from,
Establish empires of their own,
On which the sun will never rise.

Ride the Orange Bike into the Room of Surprises

Fleeing from the formless and the nameless,
We climb the sloping ramp into a boat –
A ferry that will take us somewhere
We imagine will be better, although in truth
We don't know anything about it.
As we ascend, we pass a second line
Of refugees, stumbling back
Into the time we've just escaped.

The gangway's made of
Corrugated iron, trembling
As we walk. With every step we sway,
Imagine sliding off and down.

And then, at journey's end, we leave
The ferry, eat strange cakes provided
For us, wander through a terminal,
Deserted corridors and empty rooms,
Until outside another room, we come
Upon a life-sized, cardboard
Cut-out of a person or a creature –
Perhaps an ape? – upon a bike.
The sign beneath says 'Ride the Orange Bike
Into the Room of Surprises'.

An invitation, surely, but we wonder:
Will the room be empty,
Like the rest?

Images supplied by a dream late April 2016. Title wording echoes the title of a painting I saw in 1973. It was called *'Follow the bouncing ball through the zoo-striped forest'*.

How Dreams Grow Old

As you age, the snug fit
Of life wears loose. Saturated
Colours fade to pastel:
You've developed tolerance –
Anticipated futures fail to bring
That rush you once relied upon.
They've been replaced
By a more recent addiction:
An old soak at an AA meeting,
You recount your past
One day at a time
To an audience who've
Heard it all before.

You've done the fearless
Moral inventory, stared down
Your arrogance, ignorance and
Sheer stupidity. You confer
Upon yourself the right to judge
More harshly those who haven't
Done the same, become
A sponsor of yourself, deride
Your *stinking thinking*.

You sleep less soundly now,
And the surrounding dark
Invades your dreams, where
Rooms in lit-up houses
Open windows onto black,

Dream-slopes are steeper
Than they were: beetling cliffs
With matchstick huts attached
Precariously by fraying vines.
Anywhere you tread,
Abysses open, inches
From your feet.

In the dream-kitchen,
Steam rises inexplicably from
Immaculate benchtops,
And when you yank it open,
The drawer beneath
Is full of boiling water,
Sloshing over spoons.

In dream en suites
The toilet brims with blood.
It roils and rises far too high
And will not flush away.

Nacht und Nebel

Traffic Lights in Fog

Blackheath, 24–25 April 2010

The wind blows chill across my face
From Shipley's higher ground.
Above me, tattered leaves:
Discoloured, muddied banners.

It's getting late: soon shops will close
In preparation for tomorrow's tourist tide.
The skateboard rink's deserted,
All fled except a little boy, too young
For this, one would have thought,
Who charges up and down the slope,
Gaining and losing the same ground,
While time stands still – four minutes?
Or four years?

Beneath the great dark pine
Sudden mushrooms startle with
Their thrusting caps, blood-red
And mottled, fleshy cream amidst
The drifts of dying leaves.

Cars, in columns, streaming forward,
Have turned their headlights on:
One final push before night calls
Halt to their advance.

*

The night pours rain
Upon the sodden ground.
A mist has risen, out of which
The highway lights shine sullen red.
The wind has strengthened,
Raw with wet, reminding us
That winter's waiting on our flank.

Today's the day we're called on
To remember what we never saw or felt.
A proud, pathetic column: old men,
Kids, their narrow chests decked out
With too-big medals, straggle
Towards the place of praise
And grief, its message blurred
Like traffic lights in fog.

Nacht und Nebel (Night and Mist)

Blackheath, October 2010)
See William Golding's *The Inheritors*

Night subtracts the certainties of day,
Mist multiplies the possible
To the power of n, turns friends
To strangers, strangers into wraiths.

Street lights, smudged by fog,
Irradiate a spider's web
Of wet, bare boughs,
A myriad droplets frozen
In the instant of their fall –
A zero-sum equation.

Fog refuses us asylum
In the now, repatriates us to face
The threats we fled from
There and then…

Hobbits huddle,
Cloaked against the damp,
Dubiously safe in barrows
Raised by men whose very names
Have been forgotten.

Panther tanks, black crosses
Stark against their snowy camouflage
Gallop through woods in 1944 –
Or is it 1410? The knights grind on
Across Estonia, white surcoats
Blazoned with the same black cross.

Night and fog demonstrate
Fitzgerald's Contraction, fuse
Space and time, fashion
A malleable world where
Iron becomes bronze,
Steel turns to stone, and
Intrepid adventurers,
Hunters and magicians,
(Bringing high culture to
The primitives of Ice Age Europe)
Exterminate the hairy savages
Whose lives, their leader said,
Were worthless anyway.

Snowfall

At half-past two, the swirls of sleet
Turn suddenly to snow: light, wet flakes
Spiralling and sifting in a frantic
Bid to land before they melt.

By three, the air has thickened. Now
The flakes are ponderous, settling
Like clumsy waterbirds on estuaries,
Or helicopters lifting slightly
As they graze the ground.

By half-past-three, the fall has slackened
And the ground is luminous with white,
Grass turned to wintry sea, from which
The garden beds rise starkly black
Like promontories surrounded by
An unknown, icy ocean.

The nearby tower's greyed-out,
Ghostly, a mere shadow
On the teeming air.
The heavy sky sags low,
The twigs and branches huddle closer
To the earth, the world draws in.

The wind that's blown all day
Has died away, the swish of
Snow on roofs and window glass
Is all we hear. We stare,
And smell the cold, wet air.

Wind Age, Wolf Age

In July 2011, Blackheath was close to the epicentre of a massive windstorm, with gusts of up to 140 kilometres per hour. The scenes that then ensued reminded me of the Old Norse poem about Ragnarok: the end of the world, far in the future.

Not in fifty years have such marauders
Fallen on our little town: locked doors
Torn open, roofs stripped naked,
Metal street signs plundered. Worst of all,
These Viking winds have toppled trees –
Great pines, that in a hundred years
Have grown to fifty feet, ripped
Rudely from their beds,
Their tender roots exposed.

With them went the wires
On which our comfortable lives
Depend so utterly. For four long nights
We're warped into a darker time,
A world that's lit by candlelight
And warmed by fire alone.

Now chainsaws howl like wolves.
Snow freezes on the pyres
Of chips and sawdust,
Crusts like lime on sawn-up limbs
As they await the tumbril.

Trunks still upright, crudely shorn,
Point slantwise at the sky, like giant
Cannon in a Paul Nash world, poised
To shell our certainties into oblivion.

The weather's prey to impulsivity,
Can't regulate its affect, swings its mood
From drought to flood, from blazing heat
To this, our monstrous winter.
The seas rise imperceptibly,
The glaciers are melting fast,
Rivers shrink to sullen pools.
And far on the horizon we can see,
If we are brave enough to look,
The twin towers of Asgard,
Heaped around with fuel
In anticipation of that
Final conflagration.

First Meeting with the Button-moulder

Blackheath Railway Station, Winter, 8 a.m.

Metal fuchsias pendant
From elegant curved branches,
Electric lamps stretch far
Ahead towards Mount Vic:
A city avenue in winter.
The furthest lamps, engulfed by mist
At platform's end, fade in and out of sight
As if surrendering to undefeated night.

Stark winter trees, brought here
From Bernard Buffet's boulevards,
Are ghostly presences beside the line,
Receding grey on lighter grey
Until they thin out, pass away.

The railway line itself is gone.
Look down the lighted avenue
Towards Mount Vic: the rails' dull sheen
Merges with the mist's expanding blur –
A billowing Boyg, devouring men,
Leaving behind an empty hole,
A time-warp leading only to
A kingdom of the trolls.

At his appointed time, Peer Gynt,
A man who'd made his mark
(At least in his own mind)
Returned to Norway,
Met people from his past –
Unwelcome new ones too –
Expecting each might be his last.

Our practised con-man readily
Matched wits with Lucifer;
A less impressive foe –
The Button-moulder – scared him
Shitless with the thought
Of being melted down
To dull, amorphous slag,
Without a single gleam
To show the *all-sufficient* self
He'd been.

I look again: defiant through the fog
The headlights of a train
Blaze reassuringly: it's mine:
The Mount Victoria to City
Service is on time – this time.

---

* Mount Victoria (locally abbreviated to 'Mount Vic') is the next (and last) station on the Blue Mountains line after Blackheath. The literary references are to Ibsen's poetic drama *Peer Gynt*, based on a Norwegian folktale hero.

Towards Winter

Windy Night on the Lower North Shore

In the night beyond my bed
Tangaras* honk – the mating calls
Of aluminium Diplodoci,
Summoning others of their kind
To slither their metallic length
Through this electric forest.

Sporadic gusts rattle the window.
Its loose old frames sound
Their distinctive notes, *boom-bommm*,
Like the tuned kettledrums
In Mahler's Ninth, presaging
The coming end of Earth's song.

Rain spatters uncertainly, then
Launches a frontal assault.
In the street outside, it softens
The tearing of tires
Into the swish of wings
Or fur through foliage.

When I was nine, bed was
A cave of warmth that warded off
The terror of my small, soft body
In a world of giant, evil things,
Creatures walking among us:**
My body's bigger now,
And older, but I stay
Inside the cave.

A sudden breeze fingers my face,
The curtains lurch drunkenly
Into the room, my spine shivers.
The rain has settled back
To steady dripping from limp leaves
And unseen gutters brimming
Out there in the enormous dark.

And even as
That ultimate rainy night
Draws nearer, timetabled
As surely as the next suburban train,
My warm bed, the mysteries
Beyond its margins, offer
Curious, continuing comfort:
Bomm-boom,
Boom-bommm.

---

* The futuristic Tangara-class carriages were introduced to Sydney in the 1980s

** *The Creature Walks Among Us* was a horror movie of the 1950s, the third in the series that began with *The Creature from the Black Lagoon*.

Sweet Lassitude

Some things remain the same
As fifty years ago: that sense
Of pleasant languor, absolution
From the errors of the hour,
The day – but not your life.
Collapsing easily on cushions,
Eyelids closing on the book
You thought you were enjoying,
Your aching limbs, like rubber bands
No longer taut, lie stretched and weak.

And yet it's different now.
Slipping into sleep that laps
Close by like cool, inviting water
On a blazing day, is too much
Like a forced surrender,
A flight back to the Fatherland
As red-starred tanks advance.

In childhood illnesses, my thoughts
Would wander aimlessly to pearly towers
Above the sea, explore
Some cunningly-contrived redoubt
On Crusoe's island, hidden from
Intruders by close-ranked stakes
Transformed into a glade.

Now my shining towers
Sit unprotected, my lofty balconies
Lie open to the enemy, easily reduced
From luminescent metaphor to plodding prose,
Their meanings plain for everyone to see.

I find myself beginning to
Prune back those plans
That once expanded years into
A future comfortingly indeterminate.
Snipped back like bonsai roots,
My sturdy branches shrink and gnarl.

Non-Indians, I know, prefer
The sweetened *lassi* to the plain;
But now sweet lassitude no longer comforts.
What lingers on my tongue
Is tart and sharp with salt.

Sweet Lassitude

Some things remain the same
As fifty years ago: that sense
Of pleasant languor, absolution
From the errors of the hour,
The day – but not your life.
Collapsing easily on cushions,
Eyelids closing on the book
You thought you were enjoying,
Your aching limbs, like rubber bands
No longer taut, lie stretched and weak.

And yet it's different now.
Slipping into sleep that laps
Close by like cool, inviting water
On a blazing day, is too much
Like a forced surrender,
A flight back to the Fatherland
As red-starred tanks advance.

In childhood illnesses, my thoughts
Would wander aimlessly to pearly towers
Above the sea, explore
Some cunningly-contrived redoubt
On Crusoe's island, hidden from
Intruders by close-ranked stakes
Transformed into a glade.

Now my shining towers
Sit unprotected, my lofty balconies
Lie open to the enemy, easily reduced
From luminescent metaphor to plodding prose,
Their meanings plain for everyone to see.

I find myself beginning to
Prune back those plans
That once expanded years into
A future comfortingly indeterminate.
Snipped back like bonsai roots,
My sturdy branches shrink and gnarl.

Non-Indians, I know, prefer
The sweetened *lassi* to the plain;
But now sweet lassitude no longer comforts.
What lingers on my tongue
Is tart and sharp with salt.

So Comes That Time

For Virginia Lowe

So comes that time when frailty
Confronts us bodily:
Our limbs protest like ships' masts
Straining in some ocean gale,
The cisterns of our lungs fill up
With hidden fluids, squeezing
The very breaths we draw
Into diminished space.
Our words come slowly, now,
Each one a work in progress,
Our sentences are poems, shaped
With due deliberation.

Our hearts refuse to meet
Their obligations, leak
Instead of pumping. Blood
Puddles our internal cavities
Like muddy water after rain,
Sloshing as we move.

And yet, within its creaking cage,
The flame burns clear and bright:
One final chance, perhaps, to flout
The fortune-teller's sneering certainty,
Go back on stage and claim the light,
And maybe even hear them clap
Before the hit man takes us out.

De Senectute (After Cicero)

In time gone by, I could decline
A Latin noun *(senex*, say)
Through singular and plural,
Six different terminations, signifying
Different relationships a *senex*
Might bear (hypothetically) towards
Putative Romans who might
Acknowledge him *dictator* (nominative),
Stab him (accusatively) in the back,
Appeal to him (vocative), or give
Him (dative) something he may not
Have asked for. Even the ablative
(By, with or from) had its appointed place.

I learned to conjugate a verb
(*Senescere* would do) across
The tenses, changing like so many
PowerPoint slides: past perfect
And imperfect, futures anticipated
Or ostracised to the dark side
(Subjunctive) of the Force.

Back then, the world of knowing
Seemed without a bound:
A silent ocean, bearing swells
Of ever-changing meaning
That would some day rear
One final time and charge ashore,
Impressive as the French at Agincourt,
But like them, crumple in defeat, and
Yield their standards at my surf-wet feet.

Back then, such knowledge
Seemed sufficient, justified.
But now it's me that's in decline,
My own recycled past that
Flashes by me like those slides
When a speaker's lost his way
And needs to flick back through
The frames he's overlooked.

Now it's getting in a load of wood
That seems sufficient;
Shutting doors against the wind
That spells achievement,
Finishing the washing up
In time to watch the news
That earns me a citation.

The enemy is at the gates and
Burnham Wood has come to Dunsinane.
MacDuff has drawn his sword,
The Nazgul hover close
With their unearthly screech.
Minas Tirith will surely fall,
And yet surrender is impossible.
It isn't over yet, and so
I too yell, '*Damned be he
That first cries, "Hold! Enough!"*'

I sit in a high place

Blackheath, 2016

I sit in a high place,
Secure, cossetted,
Fed by cold, mist, wind,
Hot sun, cool water.
I want for little,
Yet want much.

From this height, I look out
At truths that ramify
Before me and behind,
Yet am confined within
Uncertainties, waiting
For something more:

For the stillness of high summer,
Releasing me from clothes
Like mummy-wrappings?
For love unsought and undemanding,
Releasing me from self and doubt?
For gentle slip on bathroom steps,
Or plunge in fear from 40,000 feet?

For death, compassionate but firm,
To take my hand: '*Is that all I get?*' I ask.
'*'Fraid so,*' she says.*

---

* See Neil Gaiman: 'The Sound of Her Wings' in *The Sandman: Preludes and Nocturnes, 1995*. Death's actual reply is 'Yes, I'm afraid so.' I hope Neil will forgive the slight alteration in his wording.

Walking into rain

I step outside.
Light gleams
On flat, wet earth.
There is no wind.
A glistening bead curtain,
The rain descends
Silently into the dark.

There's no malevolence,
No savage beasts, only
This flat emptiness.
No crudely painted sign
To indicate that gas
Can be obtained,
No lighted window
Where a couple stand
Amidst the debris
Of their dream of love.

Knowing my direction,
Yet feeling no compulsion,
I walk on into rain that
Does not wet, into dark
That does not end.

Based on a dream I had sometime in the first half of 2015

www.ingramcontent.com/pod-product-compliance
Lightning Source LLC
Chambersburg PA
CBHW070924080526
44589CB00013B/1421